T0148803

COLOUR YOUR AUSTRALIA

Grace West is a Melbourne-based illustrator and book designer who grew up in Albury NSW. She loves drinking coffee, going on adventures, and most of all escaping the computer to sketch in her notebook. Grace's work communicates her love of Australia, its flora and fauna, plus architecture and iconic landmarks. North South Grace West is her online nom de plume. Colour Your Australia is her first book.

www.gracewest.com.au

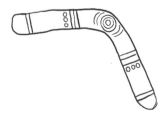

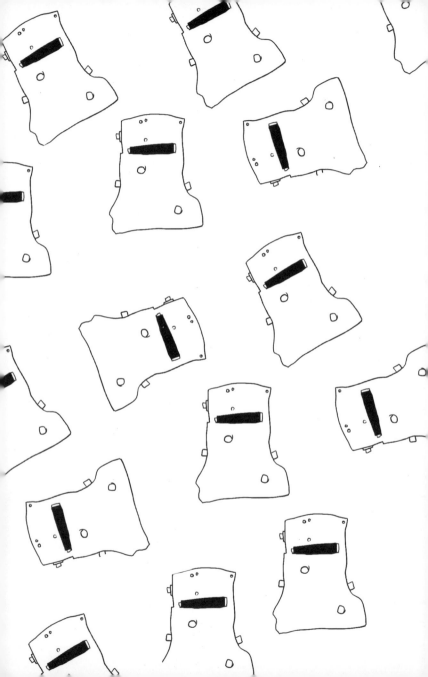

COLOUR YOUR AUSTRALIA

GRACE WEST

VIKING
an imprint of
PENGUIN BOOKS

VIKING

UK | USA | Canada | Ireland | Australia
India | New Zealand | South Africa | China

Penguin Books is part of the Penguin Random House group of companies
whose addresses can be found at global.penguinrandomhouse.com.

Penguin
Random House
Australia

First published by Penguin Australia Pty Ltd, 2016
3 5 7 9 10 8 6 4 2

Text and illustrations copyright © Grace West 2016

Cover design by Grace West and Alex Ross © Penguin Australia Pty Ltd
Typeset in Brandon Grotesque by Grace West
Colour separation by Splitting Image Colour Studio, Clayton, Victoria
Printed and bound in Australia at BPA Print Group

ISBN 9780670079339

penguin.com.au

Dedicated to my parents, Sharon and Gary,
who have always encouraged me to draw
and follow my dreams.

Australia. 7.692 million square kilometres of land, surrounded by the Pacific and Indian oceans. Home to kangaroos, koalas, goannas, platypus, echidnas, redback spiders and approximately 23 million people.

From December to February, summer in Australia is a great time to get outdoors, explore the Great Barrier Reef and Sydney's Bondi Beach, or to hike the Overland Track in Tasmania.

Autumn, between March and May, is a good time to visit South Australia for the Adelaide Festival. This season is also prime time to visit the beautiful Margaret River on the west coast, to sample some of the nation's best wine.

Australia's winter, from June to August, offers snow-sport activities in the Alps. Alternatively, this time is the dry season for the top end, a perfect time to visit Darwin for the Todd River Regatta and visit the Mindil beach markets.

Spring brings plenty of sunshine and blooming flowers in Canberra at the annual Floriade festival. From September to November, Melbourne is filled with plenty of festivals, most popularly the Melbourne Spring Racing Carnival, and the Australian Football League finals series.

I am lucky enough to have visited all eight states and territories of Australia. In another country, that could mean I'd seen most of the country. But not Australia — there are still so many places to explore. It is just so big! Each corner has its own hidden treasure and unique trait.

Common Pink Heath

VICTORIA

Queen Victoria Market

QUEEN VICTORIA MARKETS

Arts Centre

Federation Square

Melbourne Cricket Ground

Australian Open

Twelve Apostles

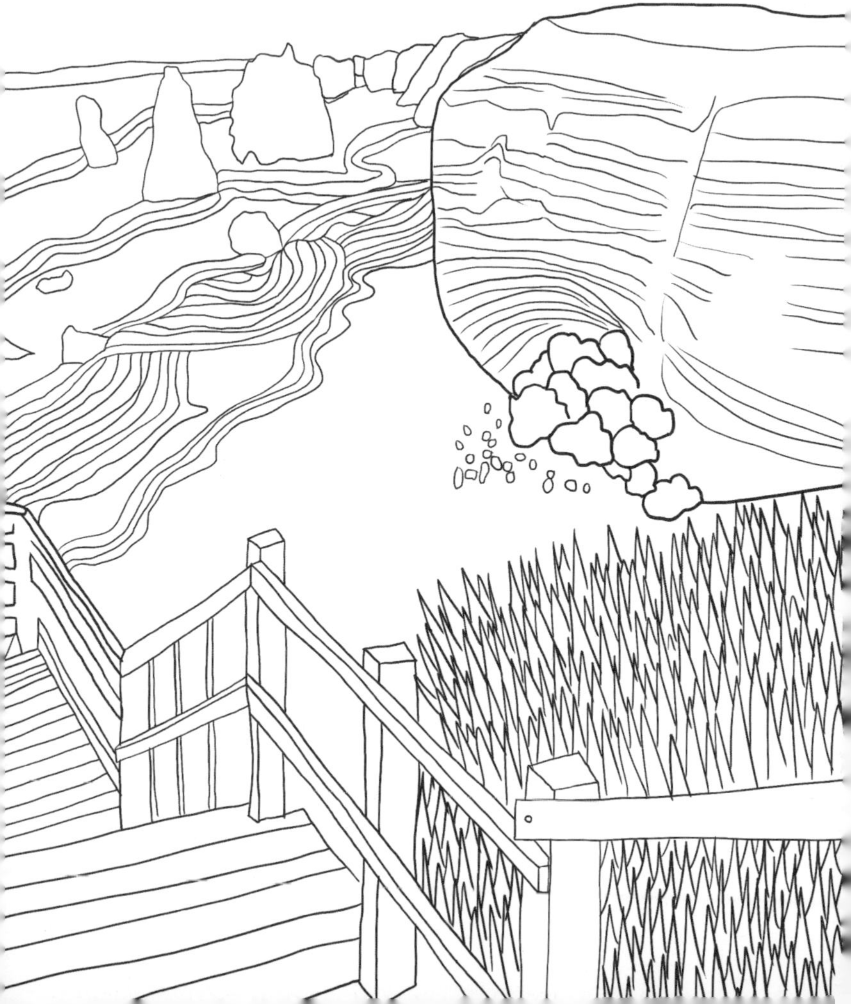

PYAP

Paddlesteamer

Puffing Billy

Waratah

NEW SOUTH WALES

Bondi Beach

Sydney Harbour Bridge

Taronga Zoo

Living Desert Sculptures

Mount Kosciuszko

Cape Byron Lighthouse

Sydney Mardi Gras Festival

Cooktown Orchid

QUEENSLAND

Daintree Rainforest

Great Barrier Reef

Birdsville Races

Gold Coast
Theme Parks

Story Bridge

Whitsunday Islands

Surfers Paradise

Turtles off Raine Island

Surf Life Saving
Championships

Big Pineapple

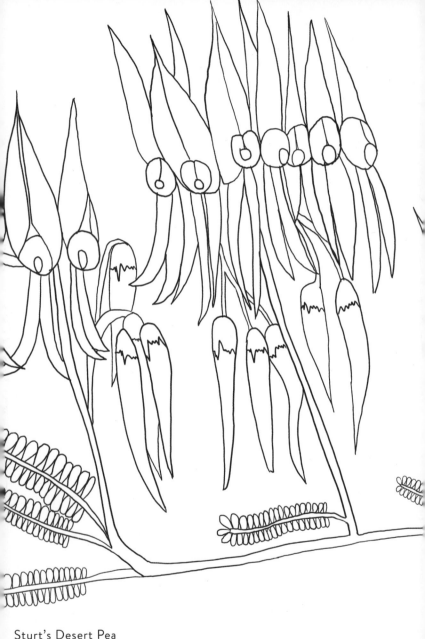

Sturt's Desert Pea

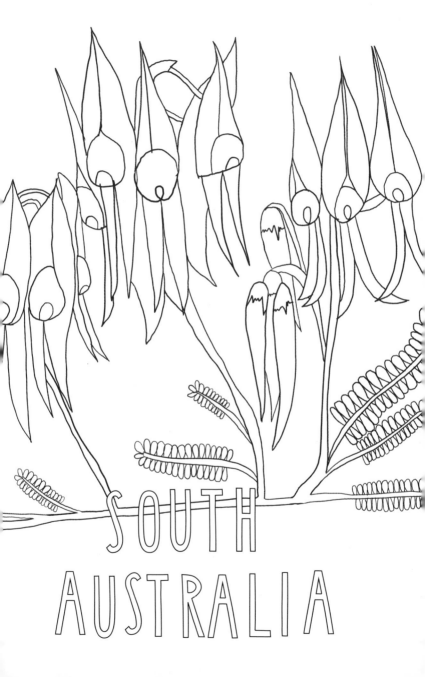

Festival Theatre

Adelaide Oval

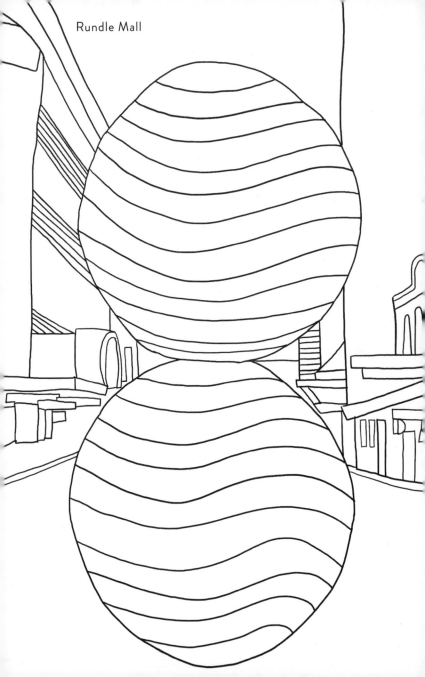

Rundle Mall

St Peter's
Cathedral

Bicentennial Conservatory

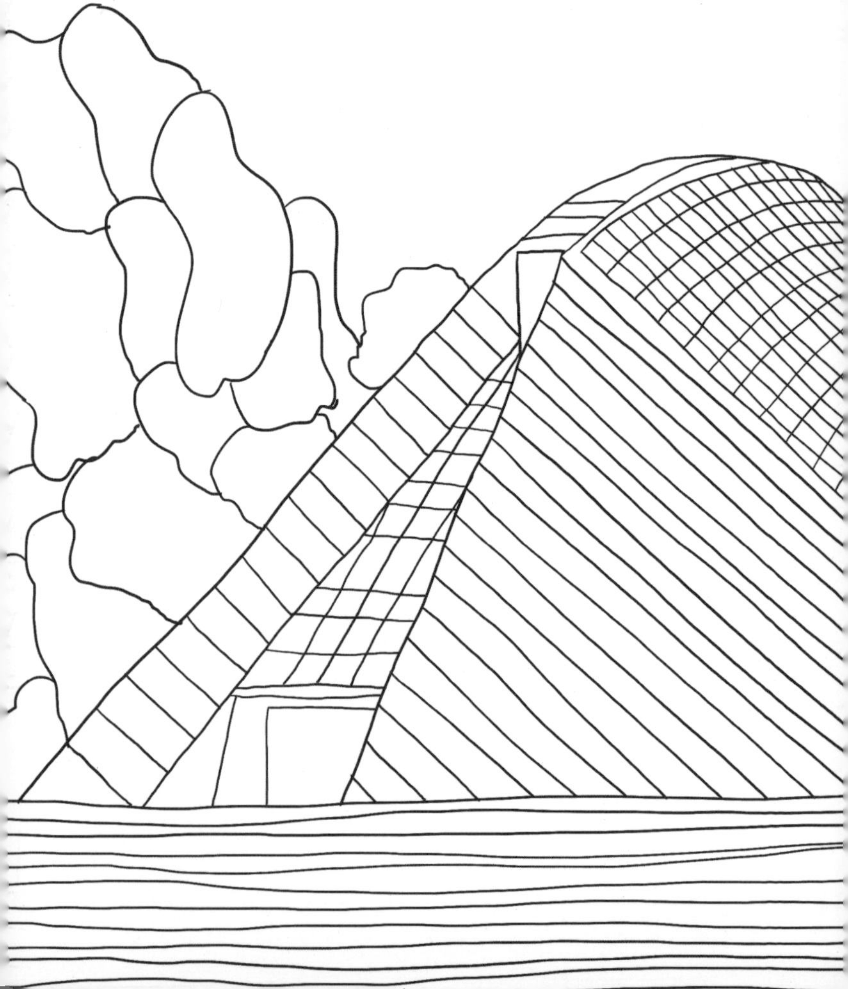

Big Lobster

DANGER

DEEP
SHAFTS

COOBER PEDY

Coober Pedy Opal Mining

Kangaroo Island

Victor Harbor Whales

Kangaroo Paws

Bell Tower

Fremantle Docks

Rottnest Island

SHIRAZ

MARGARET RIVER

Margaret River Vineyards

Wave Rock

Bungle Bungles

Sturt's Desert Rose

NORTHERN TERRITORY

Frilled Neck Lizard

Katherine Gorge

Kakadu Birds

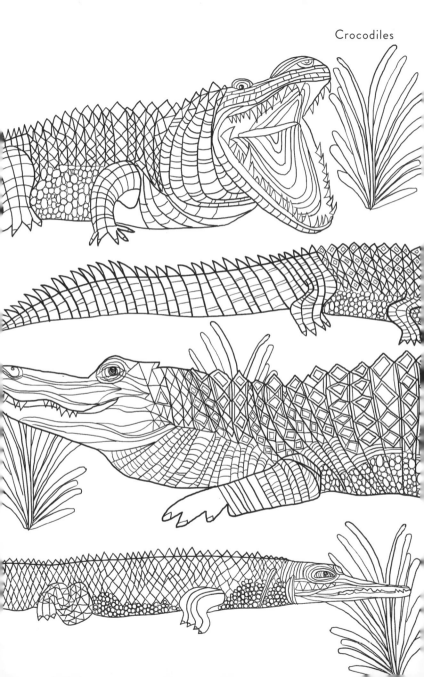

Crocodiles

Henley-On-Todd Regatta

NOODLES

BBQ SEAFOOD

Camel Riding in the Desert

Royal Bluebell

AUSTRALIAN CAPITAL TERRITORY

Shine Dome, Australian Academy of Science

Australian War Memorial

Parliament House

Canberra Bus Stop

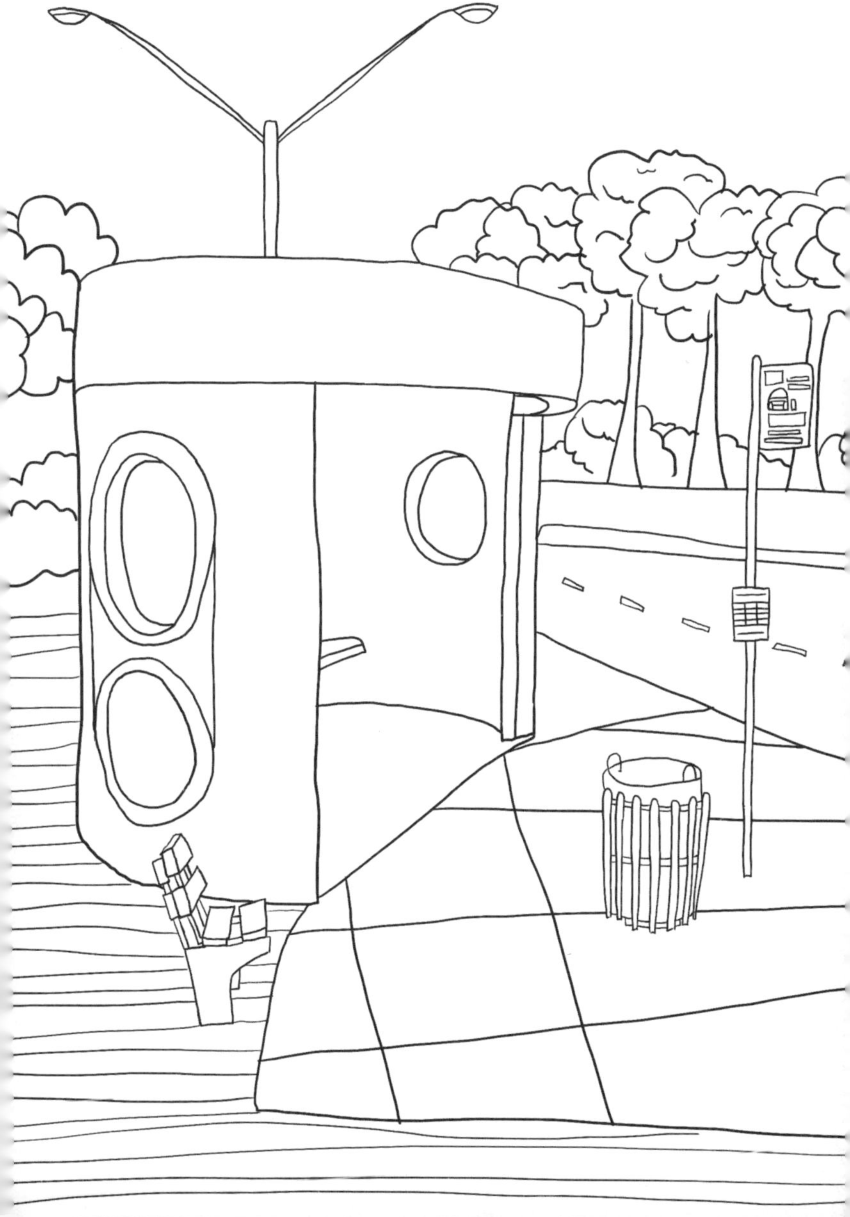

Telstra Tower

Melbourne Building

Melbourne Building

Lake Burley Griffin

Floriade

Tasmanian Blue Gum

TASMANIA

Wineglass Bay

Port Arthur

Franklin River

Spirit of Tasmania

SPIRIT OF TA

Sydney Hobart Yacht Race

ACKNOWLEDGEMENTS

Thank you to James, my partner in crime. Words don't do justice to thank you for all of your support, reassurance, encouragement, brainstorming and the multiple cups of tea and home-cooked meals.

Thank you to my family, and to my country upbringing. To my mum and dad for supplying all of those notebooks, textas, pens and paint for all those years. Thank you for encouraging me to follow a creative path. Thank you to my siblings, Tim and Court (and Andy dog), for always having faith, and bringing out the best in me.

Thank you to my cherished friends. You know who you are. Without you my little world would be far less colourful.

Thank you to the team at Penguin Books Australia. In particular, Dani De La Rue, Adam Laszczuk, Cate Blake, Fay Helfenbaum, Andrea Davison, Johannes Jakob, Tracey Jarrett and Lou Ryan. Without you, there would be no book! I am immeasurably grateful.

And to you, my colouring pal. Thank you for being creative within these pages. I hope they bring you plenty of joy. Australia is such a beautiful country; how lucky we are.

Thank you all xx

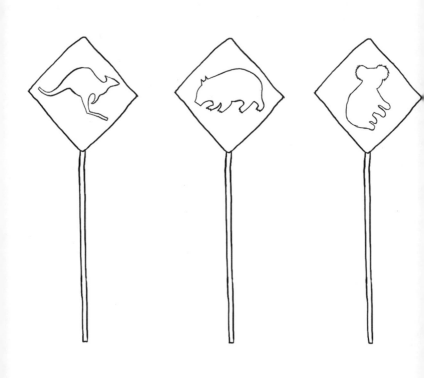

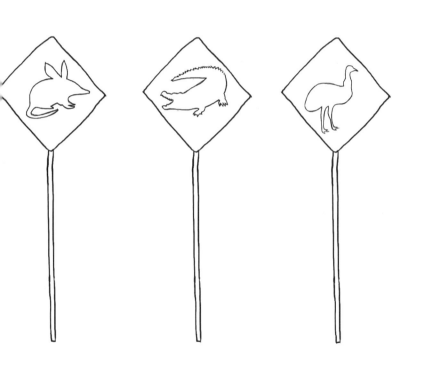